And a Sugar Bag for a Raincoat

by

Barbara Longworth
née Macadam

And A Sugar Bag for a Raincoat

All Rights Reserved

Copyright © 2016 Barbara Longworth née Macadam

Reproduction in any manner, in whole or in part,
in English or any other language, or otherwise,
without the written permission of the copyright holder is
prohibited

For information address mickiedaltonbooks@lycos.com

First Printing 2016

ISBN: 978-0-6485470-3-7

Published by The Mickie Dalton Foundation
NSW
Australia

Dedicated to you, my grandchildren, Melissa, Troy, Andrew, Joshua, Sarah, Anthony, Jesse and Madeline.

Published with love from your daughters, Susan, Robyn and Lisa

The Brush I Remember

Huge fig trees spreading their branches so high
I thought they must almost reach the sky
The gnarled roots have grown much bigger than me
And I climbed through the gaps in the trunks of those trees.

The peaceful lagoon, so tranquil, so, calm -
Weeping willows surround it to add to its charm
trees that were shrouded in mantles of vines,
Brilliant Bougainvilleas among them entwined.

Monkey vines I did swing on, it was such a thrill,
they were there for the fun as I skipped down the hill.
The heady aromas mulching leaves fallen figs
the bower bird's nest made of grasses and twigs

Fallen leaves made a carpet so soft to the tread,
or for many a small creature a comfortable bed.
The moss covered logs I passed on the way,
and scurrying creatures disturbed as they play.

The profusion of foliage, of ferns and of trees.
The coolness, the quietness, the stillness did please.
Then the kookaburra's laughter, the whip bird's call,
the bellbirds and storm birds, the owl hoot at nightfall.

Flying foxes suspended from trees all the day,
they blackened the ceiling as upwards I gazed.
Until at night they began to take flight,
to feast on the fruit trees for most of the night.

Then man in his wisdom did plunder and rape
tore down the trees and that fine covering Cape.
The swimming holes gone but the river still flows
Unheeding, not knowing what problem man posed.

Nature's Cathedral no more, naked, gaunt and grotesque:
fenced, regimental, man knew what was best
but I rejoice in the memory when nature ran wild
those memories so precious when I was a child.

And A Sugar Bag For a Raincoat

The past is not lost - it is in me - it is in you - it will be in our future generations

I have nothing sensational to write and a lot of what I remember will have been written by one person or another before. For you our grandchildren though, I want to record how it was with many things in my childhood. So as one of the girls said, "It will not be lost to them."

Living today in this wonderful technological age makes it difficult for children to understand so much; that chickens, vegetables and many other things haven't always come in plastic bags and milk in cartons or bottles. We didn't have the choice of brands in groceries, most things we bought were the basic necessities like bread, milk, sugar, flour, tea and meat. People walked, bicycled, rode horses or rode in a horse sulky instead of jumping in a car and being whisked to their destination in at times, only minutes. No television, so what did we do in the evenings? No cosy carpeted floors or air-conditioning to cool the house on those searing hot summer days which were just as hot regardless of what the experts say about global warming; and no fridges for cold drinks on demand.

So I will do my best for you our grandchildren, Melissa, Troy, Andrew, Joshua, Sarah, Anthony, Jesse and Madeline.

We lived in the country, simply, and were of an average family. A time when families were closer to the extended family than they are today. It was the normal thing rather than the exception of the present. Nursing homes were unheard of so parents and grandparents lived with and were cared for by the other family members. Perhaps there was more time in those days because we lived at a much slower pace. Though fathers had a full-time job earning a living for us all. Working mothers were non-existent where we lived, they had a full and exhaustive time running the household where mod cons were unheard of. My father worked in the bush all week, coming home Wednesday nights and weekends, so Mum coped with all the everyday traumas while sorting us kids out at times, nursing her blind and bedridden mother and caring for her father in his declining years.

Chores

We had chores to do; washing the dishes in a dish on the table and draining them on a tray to then be dried; no sink or running hot water so the dishwater was very grimy by the end of the job, it was then thrown up the backyard. The washing up table which was also used for food preparation was regularly cleaned with sand soap, an abrasive soap as the name implies; the smell I can still recall, not unpleasant.

My sister Cynthia claimed she had to polish the brass doorknobs – we had lots of doors – I don't remember that particular job though, so I couldn't have had to do that.

We helped to shine the polished lino – all the rooms had lino covered floors. We dragged each other along them on a bag, a chore that was fun. I remember when we bought a new large rug for the lounge room floor in later years, it was quite a thrill.

My brother Noel's main job (I can't remember any other) was to cut and bring in the morning wood (kindling) ready to light the fuel stove each morning. For some reason he failed to do this mostly, even with our mother's constant reminding. We girls said in later years that he was spoilt being the only boy.

Cynthia and I had the task in turns of washing our Grandfather's feet when he became too stout to bend to do them himself (no showers then.) We did them in a dish, his feet were fat and hard and the toenails misshapen. We didn't like that job, particularly when it came time to dry between the toes. But it was our job and had to be done, we did it uncomplaining.

Each weekday morning when I was old enough, I rode my bike to the butchers for the day's meat for us and my great aunt Aggie who lived up the road from us. The butcher, Danny, had a funny little poem about bee's knees and kidneys. The sawdust on the floor intrigued me and was fun to walk on, and I was fascinated by the way the butchers cleaned off the huge wooden blocks where they cut up the meat by dragging very stiff wire brushes across the surface.

The bricks on the pavement outside the shop were different to any others I have seen around town, the patterns on them were of great interest to me and I liked to walk on them. Some of them are still there today. Then back to the shops in the afternoon for other things, groceries and bread. I sometimes would pick at and eat the bread (which did not come in plastic bags), particularly at the half loaf fresh piece (where the bread was broken in half) and be reprimanded for my actions.

We fed the chooks mixing bran with water, squelching it between our fingers. I liked the smell but I didn't like the smell of the chook yard. Collecting eggs was fun but we didn't do that too often, I suppose for fear of breaking them. Sometimes we would have a clucky hen so she would sit on the eggs until the chickens hatched. Some of the chicks were very fragile so we would put them in a box near the stove for warmth, but most didn't survive this special care.

So I suppose, compared to a lot of children, particularly those on farms, we didn't have many things we had to do.

School

School was a happy time, with early memories of flowers for the teacher; asters and zinnias; counting on a bead counter, sitting on the floor and picking at each other's jumpers (woollen) and rolling the fluff into the biggest ball we could; dancing around the room on a yellow painted circle.

During the latter part of the war (World War II) long trenches were dug in the school grounds for air raid shelters and when the siren blasted we dropped everything and went to the trenches in an orderly fashion. We had many practices but thankfully no realities.

I was a good student but hated sewing, particularly in primary school. So each sewing day I "forgot" my sewing and was duly sent out into the corridor, until one day the headmaster saw me there and after finding out why I was there, sent me to third class (I was in fifth) where we played with plasticine. I was most embarrassed so was cured and remembered my sewing from then on.

Pop used to tell a story of a boy at their one teacher school (where one teacher taught several children in each grade up to high school) being in trouble, so scampered up under the schoolroom. The teacher took a pot of boiling water off the stove and poured it through the cracks in the floorboards flushing the boy out. Not a recommended procedure; imagine the repercussions today!

Uniforms were not especially uniform at our school, certainly not until high school. In primary we often went barefoot, particularly in wet weather, or wore "Roman" sandals which were brown leather with four crissed-crossed straps on the front. It was a special event when it was time to be bought a new pair. On wet days we scampered back and forth to school jumping puddles, and a sugar bag for a raincoat by tucking one corner inside the other and wearing it like a hooded cape. Some kids had rubber raincoats (no plastic then), I remember the distinct smell of the rubber as I hung my sugar bag on the hook – there were many more sugar bags than raincoats. When we got to uniforms, they were winter serge, box pleated, worn with a white blouse – winter and summer. We sweltered in the latter. When they were pressed they were first brushed with cold tea, certainly any stains were, then ironed by putting brown paper on top of the serge. In high school we wore sports uniforms (on sports day), lightweight material, box pleats, with two rows of ribbon around the bottom of the skirt; blue above red – our school colours.

I loved Empire Day (24th May) when we got a half day holiday. The morning was taken up with patriotic songs, plays and speeches. At night, bonfire and crackers. One memory of my mother working late into the night to finish a blue cardigan for me to wear for Empire Day the next day. Bonfire night was just wonderful, we spent weeks before preparing a huge bonfire, all we neighbourhood kids, using all sorts of wood and tyres (when we could get them). What excitement when it came to light it!

Some very special school times stand out; in high school being class girl captain in second form; our choir winning a section at the Eisteddfod (for which we trained extra hard), and being in the second string marching team at the district sports carnival and winning the whole competition. And when I was eleven, I went to Point Wolstencroft on Lake Macquarie on a school camp. (As I write this now, you, Maddie and Jess are actually there at this moment for a few days). This was the highlight of my school years. Train to Wyong from Wingham, passing flooded Maitland, then bus to the camp, quite a few hours journey altogether. We had a great time, games, bushwalks, sports, campfires at night with lots of songs and fun. We all cried when it was time to go home after two weeks.

I made a list of things to take with me, six pairs of bloomers, wear one; four pairs of socks, wear one; old comics, new comics. It's still a family joke – I still have the list after 54 years, written in pencil on a page of an exercise book. I spent two nights in the camp hospital with a ring worm behind one ear, visited a doctor in Wyong, so it was all quite an adventure for a quiet country kid. I remember we had nowhere to buy sweets, so we all wrote home to be sent some; our parents promptly obliged.

Mostly we went home for lunch from school but occasionally were allowed to buy our lunch, always a meat pie, Briggs pies were by far the best; carefully peel off the top layer of flaky pastry leaving a white "skin" on the top, so delicious. Even though I didn't take a packed lunch to school, I liked the smell when the other kids opened their cases with their sandwiches inside. The only school bags then were ports for girls and leather satchels that went on the back for boys.

We hopped over neighbourhood fences to go to school then up the lane beside the cordial factory where there grew a very healthy wild raspberry bush. We had many a feed of delicious raspberries over the years in our travels back and forth to school.

Things We Did

We made our own fun in those days, no electronic games, computers and the like. We played cowboys and Indians, we ran through the long summer grass with wooden guns, knives, bows and arrows strapped to our bodies ready to save the whole country from the "baddies."

One of our favourite things to do was to walk the bowling green fence – a Sunday afternoon pastime, to walk the four feet high fence on a three inch rail without falling off as it followed the contours of the uneven ground was quite a feat. What a nuisance that privet hedge was in the bottom corner, as there was no getting around it no matter how hard we tried. We always had to jump down and climb back up around the corner.

We lived almost opposite the bowling green, my great uncle George was the greenkeeper. My girlfriend Claire and I often helped him push the big roller over the green and sometimes we weeded the ditch for him. It was a long way round the four sides of the green. We were rewarded with half a bottle of ginger ale between us, often flat, probably left over from the last bowls day, but we thought it was okay.

We lived opposite paddocks that sloped to the creek; we built wooden slides to go down the grass slopes – free running – they were great. We greased the runners with dripping (fat from the meat after it was cooked); I remember sneaking some one Sunday afternoon from the container with the black-and-white checked lid, the container being on the back veranda cupboard – and getting into trouble from Mum for doing so – dripping was an important cooking commodity in those days. Today, eating or using it is a health hazard. The slides fun came to an abrupt end when one of the girls fell off the slide and broke her arm.

As kids we liked to smoke, we mostly smoked dried camphor laurel leaves (I say we invented the menthol cigarette) – in the neighbour's back shed, under the house, or in the horse stables – which Cynthia nearly set fire to once. Until we got caught, dobbed in by my friend's brother at her place. I raced home down the hill at great speed – she got a hiding from her mother – I had no repercussions but lived in fear for some days. My aunt Aggie said as I ran home, "What's the matter up there?"

I said, "I don't know, aunty," and just kept running. We never smoked again as children.

Climbing trees was another thing we loved to do, spending a lot of our time seeing just how high we could climb in the tall pines opposite our house or the camphor laurel trees at my friend's place. We were never afraid of falling, nor did our parents seem to fear for us. One time a big spider was blocking my descent in a tree and I was really scared – perhaps that is why I am scared of spiders now.

Playing around the creek was a popular pastime, always being warned not to go in the water. We did frequently but were always afraid of bullrouts with rumours (maybe it was true) of excruciating pain each sunset for a month if bitten. Once, I with older kids and decided to go across and down the creek, maybe steal a pumpkin or two off one of the farms. The creek was still swollen by floodwaters and to go in the water at that time was a no-no. So we got the pumpkins and were in the process of swimming back across the creek when we looked up the high bank and there was Mum. I got into much trouble for the adventure but we ate the pumpkins.

Bike riding was another great pastime; with mostly unsealed roads it could be difficult when the rocks would unsettle the bike. We liked to gather speed and write down the hill – no hands – my brother did this once, sped down the hill, lost control and ended up in the gully of stinging nettles. I liked to watch Dad mend a bike puncture: removing the tyre with two spoon handles and I liked to watch the bubbles when he put the tube into the water to see where the puncture was. One time, Dad had a bike to sell and advertised: he had a reply from a farmer some miles away who suggested that Dad ride the bike to the farm and there exchange it for a pig. Dad then wondered if he was expected to ride the pig home. It was a family joke for some years – "home on the pig's back."

Every Saturday afternoon we went to the pictures – ninepence (about eight cents) to get in and a few pence (known as spending money) to spend at interval on creamy toffees or chocolate when available during the war. We saw lots of serials and couldn't wait for the next week for the next episode. We watched Hopalong Cassidy. Gene Autry, Roy Rogers shooting the "baddies" in the Wild West, the Three Stooges, Ma and Pa Kettle – all in black and white. Always a newsreel before the movies and always two movies, one before interval and one after. There were lots of breakdowns during the movies, we'd sit restlessly in the dark, the boys catcalling, us all applauding when the movie resumed. The aborigines were segregated by a partition down the front of the theatre. I was scared of the ticket seller she was a cranky lady at times. As we got a little older, movies began to be shown at the Town Hall as well. These were the latest and a lot of them were in colour, so it was a real treat. At the beginning, when the MGM lion roared, we knew that we were going to be in for a treat, with an excellent movie.

I joined the Girl Guides. I liked being a Guide, Cynthia and I were in the Kingfisher patrol. We learned to tie knots, play games, went on hikes and I "promised on my honour to do my duty to God and the King, to help other people at all times and obey the Guide laws." (What the Guide laws were other than previously stated, I don't remember.) We went on church parades once a month, most Guides in our town were Church of England (Anglican) with the odd Methodist and Presbyterian, never any Roman Catholics.

One Anzac Day I was chosen to carry the guide banner in the parade. I felt so proud marching along the streets to the town Hall. We met for Guides once a week in the Scout Hall, which was at Bungay (one end of town) on the river bank. The cemetery was also at Bungay. We met at night. It was very dark, not a lot of houses or streetlights – it was rumoured there was a headless Bungay ghost – started by the Scouts. There was no way we would venture outside the hall until time for home – we had ourselves scared silly. Once on a hike down near our creek, one of the girls fell in. She took off some of her wet clothes, peeled off six pairs of pants – "Be prepared" was the Scout motto, not ours. On hikes we learned to build and light a campfire, boil the Billy and twist flour and water dough around a stick, cook it in the fire, then fill it with butter and jam – delicious.

The local council built a small swimming pool (where now stands a fine swimming centre), we called it "the duck pond," it was not very big with no filter system. But we kids thought it was wonderful. One could imagine how dirty it became, but I learned to swim in it hanging on to the sides, letting go sometimes to dog paddle then eventually striking out over-arm. I then graduated to somersaults and diving in.

We had to plead with Mum to be allowed to go at times if she thought it was not clean enough (it was emptied periodically for cleaning). Mum was right of course – it must have been a real haven for diseases. Then we were able to go to the river, Sunday afternoons at first with Dad, because he could swim, Mum couldn't. Later we went together, we kids walked through the brush (a rainforest area), swinging on the monkey vines as we went. I was always in wonder at the holly bush on the edge of the brush – I suppose I believed that holly was for England at Christmas in the cold. We still had a way to go after the brush, then we had to pick our way over the gibbers (big and small smooth rocks), which became quite hot in the sun, to get to the riverbank. One unpleasant memory was when I somersaulted off a cement pier and must have become disorientated, because I couldn't find the bottom of the river – I believed I would drown – but shot my feet out seemingly sideways and there was the bottom. I didn't somersault again for some time.

I liked to read – we read a lot of comics, which didn't do us any harm. Saturday nights we were allowed to go to the chemist shop and buy two shillings (twenty cents) worth of comics. We got quite a few for that amount of money, Comic Cuts, Radio Fun, the Phantom – my favourite, Superman and more. I liked to read books but they were not easily obtainable, but I read some schoolgirl stories and later books by Enid Blyton, also Blinky Bill. I still have a childhood book called Dalton the Dolphin. I liked to go to the library with Mum, not for children's books, always at night in the summer. Perhaps in the winter, Mum went during the day while I was at school, I don't know. Our great uncle George (yes the same one who was greenkeeper) ran the library. It had a distinctive smell – musty books I think, but I didn't mind it. I thought walking up the steps to the library upstairs was a bit creepy.

Organised sport was almost unheard of for kids except at school, but we played rounders and cricket. Rounders was a bit like baseball, we used a tennis ball and a broomhandle for a bat. Cricket was also with a tennis ball, a home-made bat and a butter box for a wicket. The boys usually batted first and when it was our turn to bat they didn't want to play anymore.

We played "Queenie" with a tennis ball. The person who was "in" threw it over their shoulder and then had to guess who had it while we all said, "Queenie, Queenie, who's got the ball?" We played "sheep, sheep come home" – someone was the fox and had to chase and catch a "sheep" before they all got "home."

We stepped out a letter game – so many steps if a letter in your name was called and double if it was a capital. The kids all got wise and wouldn't call "A" because there were too many in Barbara Ann Macadam. Hopscotch was a big favourite with us girls and the boys didn't have marbles on their own because we liked to play that as well. We played for keeps; two players put a marble each on opposite sides of the ring and whoever hit them out of the ring got to keep them. Holey was another version of marbles, with seven holes to get your marble into one at a time. In most marble games, someone was always being accused of "fudging." I remember putting all of my brother's marbles one by one down a hole in the house wall, they were irretrievable. I was not popular but he always bullied us so I suppose I was getting a bit of my own back.

"Sevens" was another game with a tennis ball, where we threw it up against the wall doing different things, starting with seven times, gradually decreasing the number of times but increasing the difficulty of what we did.

I can't remember a time when I couldn't play cards of some sort. At first, grab and old maid, then when I was a bit older, crib and euchre. I used to sit on the veranda playing cards with my Grandfather.

A popular pastime for us was to make and fly kites. Making them was as much interest to us as flying them, certainly the anticipation of whether or not they would fly was great. Put together with sticks and brown paper and held with paste of flour and water, with a tail of string and "bowties" of newspaper placed about twenty centimetres apart, we had a very good kite. We flew one so high once, that it was almost lost from sight – then the string broke.

Food

We were never really hungry except when we got home from school, but that was soon fixed with a thick slice of bread with golden syrup or jam; we never had vegemite or peanut butter. We grew most of our vegetables, our Grandfather did, so there was mostly plenty. Nothing nicer than fresh raw peas from the bushes. We grew watermelons, delicious; one of the neighbours' kids always seemed to appear when we picked and cut watermelon. We loved to run through the corn stalks which grew much higher than we were – my Grandfather called the corn, "mutti."

With no fridge in those days, meat was bought daily, we could never have been able to imagine the prepacked meats of today. We ate butter, margarine hadn't been invented – we often made our own butter, I liked it. I remember once we had bacon hanging on the back veranda, why it didn't get flyblown or go bad I don't know. The milkman delivered the milk in a horse-drawn van, the milk was in big cans and was tipped out into a billycan left on our veranda. In the summer, having no refrigerator, we used an ice chest mainly for milk, butter and perhaps leftover cold meat. The iceman delivered the block of ice carrying it with a big claw, it went into the top of the chest. Underneath there was a dish to catch the water as it melted. I often pulled the dish out at Mum's request, to check on the water level. We also had a meat safe which hung on the back veranda, used more in winter I would think. It was green, made of tin and all sides were "peppered" with tiny holes to let the air in.

The only time we ate chicken was at Christmas and Easter or when a hen went off the lay (how they knew which hen, I don't know). My Grandfather chopped the head off (which I couldn't watch) then the chicken ran around the yard for some seconds without its head (hence the saying – *running around like a headless chook*.) It was then hung up for a while then plunged into boiling water to make it easier to pluck the feathers. I liked helping with the plucking but didn't like the smell at all – I can still recall it – rather like a wet smelly dog. Then Mum would proceed to clean out the insides, sounds awful today but no one minded the job. She saved the heart, liver, neck, craw and feet and made a delicious giblet soup – sometimes we had it for breakfast. Not exactly cornflakes or cocoa pops.

We had no ice cream at home, there was neither the availability or facility to keep it, but we did have a penny (less than one cent) ice cream in the cone occasionally. Toast was made with a fork at the fire coals, tasted much better than toaster toast. I had never tasted rice until the latter part of the war (Second World War), Dad arrived home with some gotten on the black market (illegally obtained) and my first baked rice pudding was something to remember.

We always had seasonal fruit in abundance; oranges, grapes, mandarins, persimmons, mulberries, watermelons and common lemons which we kids peeled and ate with salt. On Saturday nights, my father would bring home a large brown paper bag of fruit, mainly apples and bananas which we didn't acquire seasonally. The only cold drink we had was water – straight from the tap. Cordial (fizzy drink) was only bought for Christmas. There were never any packaged drinks and juices like today – not even orange juice. We only squeezed an orange for a dose of castor oil. We did make one drink sometimes though, lemon juice with sugar and water then a small amount of carb. soda added to fizz it – quite nice but probably not very good for us. Cocoa was a popular hot drink for both adults and kids – made on milk. Tea was the main adult hot beverage though, coffee seemed to come later, to my mind it began coffee and chicory, a thick liquid in a bottle. I guess we didn't eat a lot of lollies, I remember most, creamy toffee, boiled lollies (not the imitation ones of today) and Nestles' chocolate. Only we pronounced the name differently then.

As I said earlier, we were never really hungry. Pop used to tell me a story of when he was not much more than a boy and was doing a day's droving. He lost his lunch from out of the saddle bag. So all day he had no food and this was probably from very early in the morning when he would have had breakfast. Imagine how ravenous a growing lad would be when he arrived back at the farmhouse late in the afternoon. No mobile phone to call home on and say, "Hey, I've lost my lunch, can you bring me some more?"

We ate pig's head sometimes, Mum boiled the pig's head then set it on a plate on the table – with holes where the eyes had been. I hated to look at it but I liked the taste. Rather like ham I suppose. We also ate pig's trotters (feet), they were a bit fatty but also tasted good. Saveloys were another meat we often ate, hot or cold. Sometimes we were able to buy pork fillets from the bacon factory, I think it was the best meat I ever ate as a child. Mum made delicious curries and stews, and we always had a baked lunch on a Sunday. Sometimes in the winter we ate "cubed soup" – these were Foster Clarke's – about one inch (two and a half centimetres) cube which was dissolved in water, it was quite tasty, mostly I recall tomato and mulligatawny. When our table was set for a meal the dessert spoons were always placed across, between the knife and fork at the top of them, different than today – I think it was the English setting. We always had to ask if we could leave the table when we finished our meal.

War

I was just over three years old when the Second World War started, so I suppose it was well on by my first memories. I have mentioned the trenches at school. Our friends up the road built themselves an air raid shelter, also I remember one was in the yard at the bottom hotel, it could be seen when we passed to go to the shops. I suppose there were many more in our town but we didn't have one.

My father was in the VDC (Volunteer Defence Corps), in which civilians trained to defend at home. We used to march around the veranda with a wooden gun or broom handle on our shoulder, singing, "Join the VDC and be a big galoot, wear a funny uniform and a great big pair of boots." I don't know if Dad appreciated it but he never said anything.

Some foods went on rationing – tea, sugar, butter, also clothing and petrol. The latter didn't bother us because we didn't own a car like most people didn't. Each family member was allotted so many coupons in ration books for each commodity. One day I went to the shops – I had acquired a piece of carbon paper (possessions were few) and I said to my girlfriend I would rather lose the ration book than the carbon paper. You guessed it – I lost the ration book – I couldn't have been any older than ten or eleven. I went home crying but Mum was understanding (I didn't tell her about the carbon paper), and an honest person found and returned it intact. My great aunt Aggie stocked up on a lot of tea, she had packets and packets of it stored in a cupboard and it was a family topic often.

My Grandfather's cousin lived around the corner from us, her son went missing fighting the Japanese. For three long years they waited – imagine the stress – she always believed he would come home and he did after the war, he had been a prisoner of the Japanese. He still lives in the family home today.

My father was English – he and Mum went to a dance one night and when I got up for breakfast the next morning, we had British sailors at the breakfast table feasting on steak and eggs. I guess Dad thought he had to do the right thing by his fellow countrymen.

My Grandfather was a "spotter" during the war and did shifts at the School of Arts on the balcony looking with binoculars for enemy planes. Thankfully, none were ever spotted. These men were awarded a special certificate for their war effort.

For some reason, my sister Cynthia had gone to Sydney (St Mary's) to live temporarily with our Aunty Rene. When the Japanese submarines were found in Sydney Harbour, Mum was on the train quick smart to bring her home. I suppose our parents reasoned and rightly so, that we had a much better chance in the country than the city.

My mother's cousin, Ken was fond of me, never marrying and having children of his own. During the war when he was fighting overseas, he sent me a cap of a dead Polish soldier. My mother wasn't too happy about this and eventually she burned it.

We had two aunts living in England, my father's twin sisters, Myrtle and Olive. Every now and again we sent them food parcels as they were much worse off than us with food rationing during and just after the war. The parcels were quite big, sewn up in white cloth, I know they contained tea, but what else I don't know.

One time when we were playing on the grass slopes opposite our place, a light warplane flew over us, so low with the canopy open we could see the pilot's helmet and goggles and he waved. I can still see it. Planes over our place in those days were almost non-existent, so it was a very exciting moment for us.

When word came that the war with the Japanese had ended, my mother and our friend Edie up the road, went over to the school to ring the bell – "toll out the news."

Holidays

Most holidays were spent on my Aunty Dene's and uncle Arthur's dairy farm and we had good times there. We played in the paddocks, swam in the creek, helped herd up the cows at milking time. They named a lot of the cows after us females in the family, uncle Arthur delighted in squirting us with milk from the cow's teat while he was milking and of course we would squeal and run. We kids had the job (uncle Arthur said) of shovelling up the cow pats as they happened in the yard while the cows were waiting to be milked. I wasn't much good at it and he always had to take over – it's difficult for a kid shovelling up in one fell swoop, a fresh cowpat. I know he was only kidding as when he said it was our job. I liked to watch the milk going through the pipes from the machines that milked the cows to the large vats, and where some of the milk was separated to produce cream – I still don't understand how that works.

Strangely though, with all the milk available to us when we were children, we never actually drank it. We used a lot on cereal, ate a lot of custards, and used it for hot cocoa drinks, but to pour out and drink a glass of milk was something we didn't do, not like children do today.

At first we went to the farm by horse and sulky, we

would be well loaded up and the horse would clip clop over the dirt roads, the metal wheels making a rattling sound. We went many miles to the farm, but about half way we stopped to give the horse a rest and a drink at the creek. In later years my uncle acquired a car – called it a flivver – if it wasn't a "model T Ford" it was very much like one. So then we went to the farm still quite slowly but in some style. Sometimes we went there by cream lorry, which returned the empty milk and cream cans to the farms from the local butter factory and collected the full ones to take back to the factory. The lorry left the factory very early in the morning, still dark in the winter, so we walked half an hour to the factory in the dark, just kids we were, but no one was concerned in those days, certainly not us kids. So then we sat in the back of the lorry on the wooden floor or on a cream can, the empty cans rattled and clanged the whole trip which took a long time stopping at each farm to drop off the cans.

The only boil I ever had, burst as I sat on the cans on one such trip. Boils were so painful I think bumping around burst it. (People don't seem to get boils these days thank goodness, different diet I suppose.) One time we visited a neighbouring farm down the hill, across the creek via a large log, then up a very steep hill - when we arrived there the farmer had to shot and killed one of his dogs. It had killed one of his chickens, I remember being upset about this but I suppose you could understand his point of view.

My uncle couldn't keep bull calves born on his property it being a dairy farm, so they were knocked on the head and killed at birth – another aspect of farming I didn't like. The large cans of milk and cream had to be taken from the dairy to the main road to be collected by the cream lorry, about half a kilometre. To do this, uncle Arthur hitched a horse to a wooden slide, loaded the cans and us kids and off we went. It was great fun, the slide with its metal runners going over the uneven ground, the slithering sound on the grass and the screech when it went over a rock. We clung on for dear life and enjoyed every minute of it.

My aunt and uncle rose very early in the morning to begin their day, a cup of tea and bread and jam, then off to the dairy. After a couple of hours work, my aunt then cooked breakfast and would begin her daily chores in the house then returned to the dairy mid-afternoon to do the milking all over again, then back to the house to prepare the evening meal. No mod cons, no electricity, only a woodfire to cook on – just getting the timing right with everything, particularly meals, would have been no mean feat. With no electricity, the only lighting was kerosene lamps. Hot if held too close to the face when carrying them and the glass would blacken if the flame was too high – they showed an eerie light with grotesque shadows. I'm surprised they were not more house fires in those days with the lamps and sometimes candles.

Sometimes we went to Sydney to another aunt's (Aunty Gert and Uncle Jim) for holidays, a very different holiday but just as enjoyable. The trip to Sydney then was a very long one in the train, we travelled at night, they were steam trains then, dirty and smelly from the coal. It took about ten hours as opposed to today's five. We always hoped for a corridor carriage (where we could walk up and down the carriage), and not a "dog box" where we had to stay in that carriage. I would go by myself into the city (I was about thirteen) from my aunt's at Petersham. I walked to the local railway station, up Maria Street, across Livingston Road and down the hill to the station then caught the train to Town Hall. I wandered round the shops, my cousin Val worked at Farmers and then Beard Watsons, so I "checked-in" with her while I was there. I sometimes went to a movie or a newsreel. For a few days I would catch the train from Central Station to St Mary's to visit Aunty Rene and Uncle Mick, in those days it was like a trip to the country. I always seem to be pleased to get back to Aunty Gert's, though I guess I liked the city better – but – being at Aunty Rene's in the peach season was wonderful, they had the most delicious peach tree in the back yard.

I remember one beach holiday when we camped in a tent at Tuncurry. I can only remember having an infected toe and having to be taken to Forster in a small boat (there was no bridge then) to have it lanced. The doctor gave me a shilling (ten cents) for being a "good girl." Then being flooded out a few days later, I recall things floating around in the tent. I don't think we went on any more camping holidays, I can understand why.

Church

We were a churchgoing family, except Dad, I know he was a believer but not a churchgoer. We were Church of England (Anglican). I went to Sunday school, I remember mostly the square picture stamps we got each Sunday to stick in our books. At church services we always sat in the same pew (still do, I suppose) and the local dentist's wife sat in front of us. She wore a fox fur stole, the head, tail and paws hung down her back. Being a kid I was at eye level with the fox's eyes, I didn't like that. I didn't like the smell of the wine when the adults came back from communion. I remember when I was old enough, going each Wednesday afternoon after school to the church for confirmation lessons. Then being confirmed in a white dress which doubled for wearing to the local annual agriculture show. We mostly had a new dress and sometimes new shoes for the show. We had scripture lessons at school, I recall it in high school.

We had scripture exams, I took it seriously and got an honour certificate one time, but some of the boys clowned around a lot. When asked one question to complete the line, "*There is a green hill far away,*" one boy wrote, "*where Wallabies roam.*" The Reverend wasn't impressed. We didn't have any communication with Catholic kids in our town, they could almost have been on another planet. My Grandfather was very bigoted against the Catholics as indeed they would have been against us. Thank goodness it is not so today.

The Reverend was quite a figure around town, often wearing his long black gown, leather belts and biretta. Pop remembered most his big driving gloves. He drove fast – someone said to him that he did – he replied that the Lord is with them – only to be answered that it was a wonder that the Lord could keep up with them.

When I was older we went on church parades with the Girl Guides as mentioned before. We always seemed to get the giggles over something or other, it didn't take much to set us off. When older, I joined the Fellowship, we met in the Oddfellows Hall, had lots of fun, played car hide and Seek around the town, and held dances. I suppose all these things to do with church association laid the ground work for me with religion. As children we went to church because we were made to and a lot of adults went because it was a social thing (for some, anyway.) I believe most people who go today do so because they want or need to – as it should be.

Christmas was a special time but not commercial as it is today. I don't remember a lot of presents, certainly we would have received only one thing. A black doll comes to mind (Topsy, which eventually became khaki as the black flaked off), a rubber beachball, a dinky – for Helen probably. When I was eleven I got my first watch for Christmas, I treasured it, couldn't stop looking at it – I still have it though of course it doesn't work. On Christmas Eve (afternoon) we were given some money to go downtown to spend it how we liked. One year I bought my Grandfather some hair oil as a present – he was bald, and my father a book of English poems because he was English – Dad was a reader but not into English poems, so that went back to be exchanged – I guess the thought was there. We had a great roast chicken dinner (lunch) followed by plum pudding in which we hoped to find some threepences. Always cordials and cherries. Easter was a nice roast chicken lunch, with nothing else for celebration. Easter eggs were not heard of in those days.

Miscellaneous

As children we didn't have many toys but amused ourselves without any trouble. I did have a celluloid doll dressed in white baby clothes. The clover in our backyard grew about twenty centimetres high, so I could make a bed for the doll in it and sing, "White Christmas" to it – my Dad sang that a lot around the house. Alas, the doll was lost when it caught fire at the fuel copper in the laundry and was gone in a flash.

Our fires were all wood, the kitchen stove, the copper for doing the laundry and the open fire for warmth. It was nice to sit beside the open fire with the family on a winter's night. On very cold mornings it was lit also, great to get dressed for school near it. I learned to knit sitting in front of the fire, watching the knitting grow every few rows. My brother Noel tried to knit when he was a little fellow, but cried when he dropped a stitch – I guess he thought it would be lost forever. We also did French knitting with a cotton reel with four tacks on the top, winding the wool around them and lifting the wool over itself and the tacks until it grew long enough to come out the bottom of the reel. The only trouble was we didn't know what to do with this long tube of knitting or what purpose it could serve – I still don't.

With no television in those days we listened to the wireless (radio) at night – *"The Search for the Golden Boomerang"* (I don't know if it was ever found), and *"The Amateur Hour"* on a Sunday night. Dad listened to the cricket, the radio would crackle. I remember sitting on the floor beside his chair listening too. Being English, Dad would want them to win. I felt sorry for him being on his own in that, so I wanted them to win too.

Dad was a smoker, sometimes he would go to a pipe – after a time his pipes had to be "sweetened" (for some unknown reason) – he tried boiling them in milk, then another time heard that burying them for a while was the thing to do. Well he did this but when it was time to dig them up he couldn't remember where he had buried them – Mum was highly amused. Sometimes Dad combined different tobaccos in a jar, probably to get a better blend. One night our church curate came to listen to the cricket with Dad (not everyone had a radio, I would say especially not a poor curate). Dad gave him a cigarette rolled from the jar blends. Later Dad asked him if he would like another cigarette. He said, "No, Mr Macadam, that will do me for a very long time." Too strong for him, I would say.

We had no luck with dogs – any we acquired seem to end up frothing at the mouth and dying – no vets in those days. Once we had a cow – I was scared of it and it didn't seem to like me. It bailed me up in the toilet which was quite a way up the backyard from the house and Dad ended up breaking my brother's cricket bat over its back trying to get it away and rescue a screaming kid.

I liked it when the creek flooded. At first it would just be visible, then as the rain kept falling, the creek became a raging, muddy torrent carrying trees and sometimes dead cattle along with it. I was fascinated. I always hoped it would come up enough to cross our road but it never did. Once it almost made it to the fence on the other side of the road – close. Sometimes at night in the summer there would be a foul smell wafting in the air – one of the adults would be heard to say that there must be a dead cow in the creek. No one worried about it and after a few nights the smell would be gone – all just a normal occurrence. Just as well the creek flooded sometimes though, to clean it all out.

We didn't go to the doctor much in those days, not like people do today – were we healthier? The word virus was never used. We got boils, though not a lot in our family – we hardly ever hear of them today. Stone bruises were prevalent, a product of not wearing shoes much and most of our roads were unsealed – didn't it hurt when we trod on a sharp stone! The stone bruises came up like a boil on the soles of our feet and had to be drawn with a poultice of flour and water and heated on the fuel stove to hot as we could stand – a painful process all round. We had lots of nosebleeds, I remember having a week in bed taking some foul tasting medicine for a cure; I don't know if it worked – grew out of it like all kids I suppose. My mother used to suffer with heart palpitations and had to lie down when this happened – I remember lying beside her hoping she wouldn't die. She also had something wrong with her that she couldn't walk properly, the doctor advised her to learn to ride a bike – she did and eventually got better.

Death in humans we didn't think about as kids until the reality arrived. On neighbour's little girl died of diphtheria, never having been vaccinated as we were. The neighbourhood was devastated. Then one night my Aunty Dene and Uncle Arthur from the farm arrived with their few months old baby, Brian, dead in her arms – she had held him on the long trip from the farm, one can only imagine what must have gone through their minds – it was probably a cot death. They laid him in the room next to where I was supposed to be sleeping; I remember lying in the dark thinking about him. Several years later the same family lost their three-year-old daughter with peritonitis, again arriving at our place with the desperately ill little girl. She was operated on but died. Too much for any parent to bear. They lie side by side in the country cemetery between my father and mother and our maternal grandmother. Our family couldn't understand why for so many years they lay in unmarked graves but I think the hurt was too great to cope with anything more. Two years later my father became ill and after my mother nursed him for eighteen months, he died quite suddenly. Then one year later, my Grandfather who lived with us all my life, died suddenly also as I sat in the room with him. Death was surely a reality. I only know now how much my mother must have suffered during and after these times. My Grandfather always maintained that when his first wife died, he was working in a field and a woman in black stood momentarily beside him; when he returned home his wife had died. I don't know what to say about that, but Grandfather was an honest enough man.

We had no shower for bathing, though our friends up the street eventually did – it was heated by a chip heater. I was intrigued by it. We bathed twice a week, us kids following each other into the bath with a top up of hot water each time it was someone else's turn in the tub. The bath was tin, the water heated in kerosene tins on the fuel stove. They must have been extremely heavy to lift from stove to bath as they were quite large. The nights we didn't bathe, we washed in a big tin dish; I can recall sitting on the bathroom step with the dish on the kitchen floor, washing myself, particularly washing the sticky ergot (grass) off my legs.

Then came our chip eater, what bliss! It was a round tin device with a fire made with wooden chips in the centre, surrounding that was the water which of course heated very quickly. The heater huffed and puffed away giving very hot water, I was always a little afraid that the heater would blow up the way it puffed and puffed. It also heated the bathroom and was great in the winter. The bathroom wasn't lined so it was normally very cold in winter with the cold air drifting through the cracks and knot holes in the walls. So what luxury we had come to! I suppose Mum thought so too in more ways than one for, for starters not having to lift the heavy tins off the stove.

Telephones were quite a luxury when I was growing up but eventually we got one. On Saturday afternoons an SP (starting price) bookmaker used it to take bets (an illegal practice but widely accepted), so we would have been paid for that. Occasionally he wouldn't turn up and the adults could be heard to say that the "D's" (detectives) were on their way from Newcastle (we lived north of Newcastle). So the word was out – I guess not many bookies were caught with that sort of network. Sometimes there was a bit of a flurry on when the bookie had taken too many bets on the one horse and so had to "lay it off" with another bookmaker – all very technical stuff.

Divorce was hardly ever heard of in our growing up – if you were a divorced woman, you must have had a reputation and were something of an outsider in most social circles. A male cousin of my mother's got divorced, he was quite the topic of conversation in the family at times. People didn't "live together" like today, it was unheard of and to rear a child out of wedlock was almost a disgrace. A distant relative who lived near us did just that, what courage she and her family must have had to stand firm in the face of a condemning community. Even we as children, playing with the boy each day, thought of him as "different."

My friend's mother was often rousing at her children, so mostly I gave her a "wide berth." One day we had to go to the post office to post a letter for her. There was a well in the backyard of my friend's house, boarded over the top. My friend poked the letter through the cracks in the board pretending to drop the letter into the well – you guessed it – down went the letter into the well by accident. We were too afraid to tell – I mean, how difficult would it have been for her mother to write another letter? So we spent the two pence (about one and a half cents) for the stamp, we didn't mind that bit though. I suppose it was always a mystery why the aunty never answered the letter.

I had curly hair, almost shoulder length and every morning it was a traumatic experience to have it done for school. We didn't have hairbrushes, (well we didn't), conditioner was unheard of, and we washed our hair with Sunlight soap (laundry soap.) Our hair was always nice and shiny but to have it combed, to say the least, was painful. Then Mum put Curlypet on it (probably to help keep the curls in) which smelt very pleasant – I can still remember it – and then roll the hair in sections round her finger to make sausage curls – cute. In winter, if we didn't have the open fire on, we would stand at the back of the house with our backs to the brick chimney to get the warmth of the sun on the brakes while the hair "operation" was done.

My Grandfather went fishing in the river. I was fascinated when he would lift the long boards at the back of the house and there would be quite a number of long flat worms for bait. On Fridays we often ate fish though of course we were not Roman Catholics who ate fish every Friday – meat being against their religion on that day. We had Catholic neighbours who fished Thursday night (don't know where) and I was often sent to their place Friday morning before school to buy some fish for us. I recall baskets of fish in their back yard for us to buy from.

Mum liked fresh flowers in the house. If she didn't have any of our own to pick she sent me to a neighbours up the back of us to buy some. A widowed lady with a nice garden; there I would buy six pence (five cents) or nine pence worth of flowers and got a good bunch. Another pretty thing to put in a vase was gum tips – the new tips on gum trees which had a reddish tinge. Mum grew quite a lot of flowers in season (I didn't take after her for gardening), zinnias, asters, poppies, snapdragons and stocks. We had cannas and arum lilies growing "wild" on the cool side of the house. It always seemed damp there, probably the bath water drained there. One time we had a nice bed of poppies in flower which attracted a lot of bees. One Sunday morning while Mum was at church I got an empty tobacco tin and try to catch the bees on the poppies – ruined all the flowers. Mum was not pleased when she arrived home – I can still see the bed of bedraggled poppies.

When I was ten I realised that Mum was going to have a baby. I didn't know anything about that sort of thing, except some boys told us once that babies came out of the bellybutton and I believed that. In those days children were not told about additions expected in the family. Today I think they know almost as soon as the parents. I felt sorry for Mum, don't ask me why, so every Saturday afternoon when I went to the pictures I brought her home a chocolate out of my spending money. Almost certainly I would have used most of it for her but I never even thought about that – it was something I wanted to do. So when the time came and Mum went to hospital, Dad and Grandfather sat on the veranda into the night waiting for the news of the birth – fathers didn't go anywhere near the hospital during the birth in those days.

Mum had a hard time when I was born, so with that in mind they would have been more concerned. So Helen arrived, we all thought her a little miracle – so tiny. I used to walk to the hospital after school to visit them, it was quite a walk from our house. One afternoon, the man whose wife was in the same ward as Mum offered me a lift in his truck when I was going home, but I was too scared to get in – even then we must have been aware of "stranger danger." I remember the adults having a bit of a giggle about it as they knew the people quite well. Helen always seemed to have trouble gaining weight as a baby and Mum and Dad were always concerned about it. I felt relieved after they visited the clinic and Mum would say that she had gained some weight, even if it was only a couple of ounces. Now, like all of us, I suppose she wishes she could lose some.

I had never tasted bubblegum it wasn't available until well after the war. My sister Cynthia had gone to Sydney for a holiday and brought back quite a lot of it as it was just on the market; it was Goblin bubblegum. I thought it was great and was thoroughly enjoying it when suddenly we were in the midst of a polio epidemic which was widely spread. There were no preventative vaccines then. Rumour had it that it was spread by blowing bubbles with the bubblegum – alas, it had to be destroyed as polio was a devastating and crippling disease. I watched with dismay as Mum burned every single stick of it in the wood fire. I don't ever remember having bubblegum again after that.

We weren't a musical family, though Dad sounded okay when he sang around the house and Cynthia has a good voice and sings in choirs. But we kids thought we were pretty smart when we "discovered" the comb and paper instrument, by putting tissue paper over the comb and blowing the tunes through it, it sounded good to us. I also tried "playing" a gum leaf but couldn't master that, I think it took some skill which obviously I didn't have.

My friend Claire's family had a windup gramophone, which we played often. As far as I know there was only the one record, *"Jimmy Cracked Corn,"* which we played over and over. The needle had to be changed every few plays and if it started to run down while it was playing, it sounded terrible until we gave it a few winds. We had lots of fun with it. When we got our first radio gram (electric record player) a few years later, we thought it was wonderful. A Donald Peers record was the first one I remember us having.

A woman came to town and started dance classes, which I joined – tap and I suppose jazz ballet. I thought I was "Christmas." Friends of ours in Sydney whose daughter did dancing brought some of her discarded costumes and gave them to me and I thought I was "Christmas" again. They were kept in the "top room" wardrobe, the long drawer at the bottom, above which was a long mirror. One costume had a taffeta cape, white one side, green the other – I loved to put it on and dance around in front of the mirror. There was also a sword dance costume and I pranced around doing this as well. The dance teacher put on a concert in the town hall and I remember we danced to *"Begin the Beguine."* Mum and Dad weren't impressed with the whole thing and I seemed to give up dancing not long after that. I would never have made a dancer, but I loved the clacking of the tap shoes.

As I said earlier, we were not endowed with possessions, nor lots of clothes. My first dressing gown (chenille) belong to my Aunty Vi who had died – she was tiny – I was about eleven. I would run my fingers between the rows of chenille – I was so happy with it, but didn't know then where it had come from – not that it would have mattered to me.

We were bought slippers as needed, we girls, it was great when it came time for a new pair. They had a pom-pom on top. Sometimes Mum would find a flea in a pom-pom, fleas were around more so then – I can still see her searching through the pom-poms.

We lived with my Grandfather, he owned the house. it wasn't all that big I suppose, but had three bedrooms with verandas around half of it. My Grandfather and my brother Noel slept in the "top room," also called the boys' room at the front of the house, which had a three-quarter bed for Grandfather and a single bed for Noel. Cynthia and I slept in a double bed in another room, which opened onto the side veranda; the windows opened onto the front veranda. Mum and Dad (and later, Helen) slept in the room opposite the lounge dining room, closest to the kitchen. In the kitchen which was quite big, we also ate our meals as it contained a dining table.

The fuel stove was at one end of the room and the open fire on the back wall. Both this room and the lounge room opened on to verandas; the kitchen also had a door to the bathroom and a door on the back wall, which opened outside – then we walked across the long boards to the laundry. In summer we often slept on the veranda; my Grandfather always did. It was great except for the mosquitoes. Sometimes on a really hot summer's day, we would lie in the hallway on the lino (no carpets then) which was cooler – I remember my uncle on the farm doing that a lot. Grandfather willed the house to his youngest son and not too long after he had died we had to move as my uncle Harry wanted to sell it. It hardly seemed fair on Mum with two of us kids still at home and having looked after her ageing mother and father. So we moved into a housing commission place up the road. Round the corner and down that road. It probably did us a favour in the long run – a more modern house – but we didn't think so at the time.

So many things we didn't have – no television, phone (later), washing machine, electric jug, toaster, no air-conditioning, no backyard pool, skateboards, surfboards, transistors, tape or video recorders or DVDs, no mobile phones. We didn't have motor mowers or whipper snippers. Hardly any cars – we walked a lot or rode a pushbike. Clothes were of a minimum, no tracksuits, joggers or the like – we would be lucky to own a pair of ordinary sand shoes. Take away foods were unheard of – except for the local cafe, shops closed at five o'clock and sometimes for lunch – and were closed Saturday afternoons and all day Sunday. Shopping malls were not in existence, except for several small ones in the city. No water toilets, particularly in the country: it was a pan toilet some yards up the back of the house, with a pan being emptied weekly. It's a wonder we didn't get a lot of diseases from it – I couldn't go back to that again. We didn't have the pressure of drugs or sex problems; I never heard the word until I was almost grown. We weren't "latchkey" children, hardly anyone was back then; to come home each day from school to Mum was a secure feeling.

So we raced through our childhood in the fantasy of movies; Tarzan swinging through the jungle trees, pirates swashbuckling and boarding ships, plundering their treasure (I wonder where all that treasure came from), the losers having to walk the plank. Cowboys and Indians with Gene Autry, Roy Rogers and Hopalong Cassidy – and the

MGM lion roaring to herald another great movie. No matter what movie I saw, when asked by Mum what it was like, it was always "good." The comics we read each week – *"Mandrake the Magician," "Superman,"* my favourite, *"The Phantom" (The Ghost Who Walks), "Comic Cuts"* and *"Radio Fun."* We scrambled the creek banks, waded the creek, slithered down the grass slopes on our slides. We raced through the long ergot grasses by day and warm summer evenings with wooden guns, knives, swords and bows and arrows strapped to our bodies.

At one time for a few months, a roller-skating rink was set up in town and that was our main attraction for that time. We took school in our stride, hardly missing a day or wanting to. We enjoyed all that we did, made mud pies after the rain with the special smoothed mud in front of our house and couldn't understand why they cracked and broke when we tried to dry them under our house. Made and flew our kites, played our ball games and rode our bikes. Had good holidays whether it was farm or city. And above all, always felt secure within our family and extended family of which they were aunts, uncles and cousins in abundance. It wasn't until death came into the safe order of our family that I began to realise that things do change and nothing lasts for ever.

I have described things as they really were with no exaggerations. I think our growing up was exciting and interesting, but I'm not saying I would like to go back to that way of living. Advancement in almost all things over the years must surely be for the better. We were not a slave to the clock and lived a much slower pace – for that reason we mostly "took in," understood and appreciated what and why we did what we did. The adults worked hard – today too – but harder physically in those days.

By reading this, I hope you, the fresh new generation can understand our different attitude to yours about many things. We were much more down to earth through necessity, were closer to nature. Realising how it was with us should help you understand us as we try to do the same with your generation; though the generation gap is a natural thing – perhaps we learn from each other. We have given you your way of living, the good and maybe the not so good – but at least you will never have to wear A SUGAR BAG FOR A RAINCOAT.

Some Old Pictures

NATIONAL FITNESS COUNCIL OF NEW SOUTH WALES.
MACQUARIE AND BENT STREETS, SYDNEY. TELEPHONES: BU 3331, BU 3332, BW 2291.

TRAVEL AND GENERAL INFORMATION FOR THE GUIDANCE OF SCHOOL CHILDREN ATTENDING BROKEN BAY OR POINT WOLSTONCROFT NATIONAL FITNESS CAMP

Master/Miss *Barbara Macadam*

Your application to attend Broken Bay (Boys) or Point Wolstoncroft (Girls) National Fitness Camp, having been accepted, the following general information is supplied to facilitate your travel and help you to enjoy your experience.

TRAVEL.

TRAVEL.

Forward Journey.

Inquire at local station concerning exact time of departure of train which arrives Central 7 a.m. on Friday, 12th August.

Join train at local station Thursday, 11th August.

Return Journey.

Depart Central 8.15 p.m. on Friday, 26th August.

Inquire at local station concerning exact time of return journey.

Boys will travel to Palm Beach by bus.
Return fare - 10d. - then by ferry to camp - no charge.

RATION COUPONS.
These must be of issues current during the camp period and should be enclosed in an envelope on which the name, address and ration book number of the camper should be written. TEA—2 coupons; BUTTER—1 coupon.

CAMP REQUIREMENTS.
Each camper should have—Mug and two plates (of durable material; one plate should be deep dished for soup and like dishes), knife, fork and spoon (these to be kept in a linen bag), two sheets, one pillow case, two bath towels, one tea towel, soap and toilet articles, underwear, pyjamas, a warm cardigan, socks, sandshoes or sandals, an old pair of leather shoes and a raincoat or cape, one exercise book and pencil, stamps, envelopes and stationery.

GIRLS.
Swimming costume and cap, playsuits or shorts and shirts. A sunhat. DO NOT BRING UNNECESSARY JEWELLERY.

BOYS.
Trunks, shorts and shirts.
Optional: Torch, camera, musical instrument and fishing gear.

ALL CLOTHING AND OTHER ARTICLES SHOULD BE CLEARLY MARKED WITH THE CAMPER'S NAME

CAMP BANK.
Valuables, pocket money, train ticket and ration coupons are to be handed to the Camp Instructors immediately upon arrival. Only sufficient money for fares and incidental expenses on the forward and return journeys plus a maximum of 10s. for pocket money while in camp should be carried.

The Department of Education and the National Fitness Council are confident that your stay in camp will be a happy and profitable experience of which you will tell others in the cause of National Fitness.

MONEY

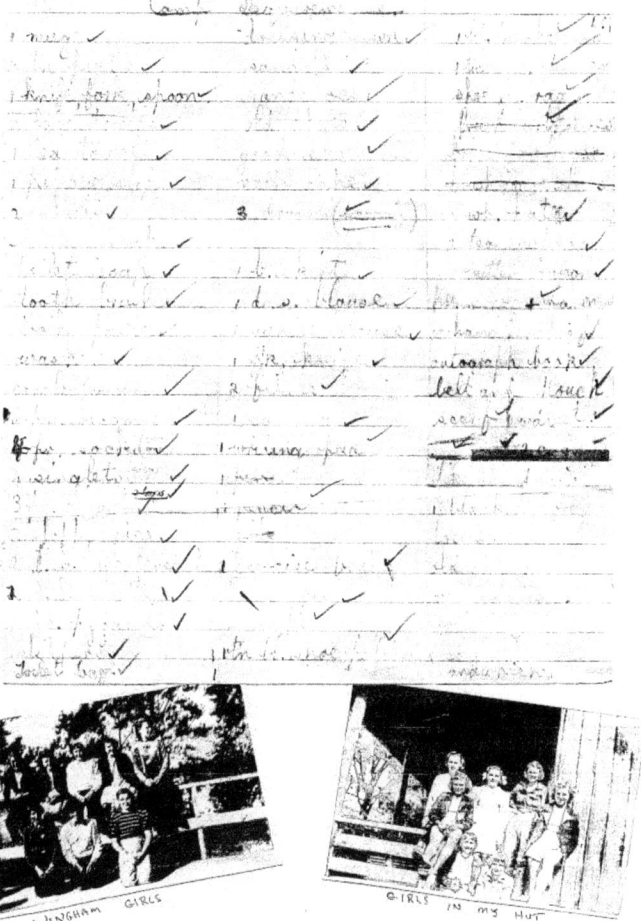

WINGHAM GIRLS

GIRLS IN MY HUT

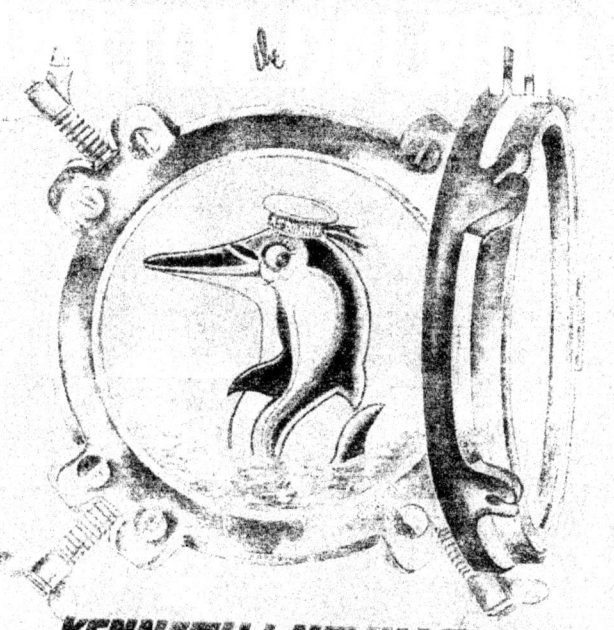

THE GREVILLEANS

WINGHAM GIRLS

MESS HALL

JILL MACGREGOR

OUR HUT

SISTER PODMORE

LAKE MACQUARIE

Below: The Wingham butter factory.
The Wingham and Upper Manning District Co-operative Butter and Bacon Company Limited commenced operations in 1907 and at its peak had some 300 suppliers. In 1919 there was also a branch factory at Bobin. The factory manufactured butter under the "Mannabah" and "Allowrie" labels and in 1960 won eleven of the thirteen first prizes for butter at the Sydney Show. The factory closed in 1979.
Photo: Dick Budden, Wingham.

SCHOOL SNOW
No "snowmen" are in sight but it was reported that Brinawa school students built some when their school was in the centre of a heavy fall of snow — M V Historical Society

POP'S SCHOOL

St Matthew's, Wingham, and the new Church complex.

MACHIN'S AT ELANDS
Henry Machin set up this timber mill at Elands in 1915 to cut axe handles. The site was later used as a mechanic's shed in a building constructed by Machins — John Machin

MY FATHER WORKED AT THIS MILL.

MACHIN'S SECOND TIMBER MILL AT ELANDS
Machin's second mill at Elands with Henry Machin in front of the logs. This steam driven mill worked until 1957 and contained a No 1 and No 2 bench. Logs up to 17' in girth were broken down

TINONEE ROAD - WINGHAM IN BACKGROUND

Bent Street in Wingham about 1922 contained many buildings that still stand today. The streets were of gravel.

BENT STREET - WINGHAM

Cedar Party Creek bridge into Wingham was completely submerged in the drastic 1929 flood.

The 1929 flood in the Manning River inundated Primrose Street in Wingham. Residents survey the damage on the 9th February.

www.ingramcontent.com/pod-product-compliance
Ingram Content Group UK Ltd.
Pitfield, Milton Keynes, MK11 3LW, UK
UKHW021045200426
11947UKWH00036B/1023